Yff's Theory of

Mandatory Social Accountability (MSA)

by

Larry A. Yff

CHAPTERS

2

INTRODUCTION

There are many theories and writings about social responsibility in circulation, but what separates this one from most is the fact that it's based on the premise that humanity's accountability to a non-human entity is mandatory and supersedes its' accountability to society, whether we like it or not.

This accountability allows for the human process of establishing rules and regulations in society to provide the maximum social benefit and extract the maximum potential from all of society's members SO LONG AS it adheres to the rules and regulations set forth by a non-human force.

What follows are the 3 core principles of my theory along with 3 important definitions:

CHAPTER ONE

<u>Mandatory Defined</u>

Mandatory is official. Mandatory is something that you *have* to do. It is an undeniable *something*. In order to grasp the true meaning of mandatory, we will look at it outside the parameters of modern society because modern society has a way of shaping what mandatory is to fit its' will. It should not be able to be conformed to any one person or society's will. It should be able to be universally applied to all of humanity, for better or for worse.

Let's look at it in the true legal sense of the word. The act of being mandatory provides the most powerful legal basis of action or statements. If something is mandatory, it means that whatever it is legally being applied to is not pliable. It is not up for debate, discussion or dispute. It is the unchallenged and unquestionable law.

Let's switch gears and look at what mandatory is in nature. In nature, everything is held in place by natural law. Natural law reigns supreme and holds court over human life, animal life, plant life and inanimate objects.

If you throw something into the air, it will come down.

If you touch fire, you will get burned.

If you combine 2 parts of Hydrogen with 1 part of Oxygen, you will get water.

If you stand outside when it rains, you will get wet.

If your lungs stop getting Oxygen, you will die.

The longer you live, the closer to death you will be.

Do you see where I'm going with all of that? There are things that are mandatory. They will happen. They *have* to happen if you do certain actions.

I believe, and society tends to show it whether it acknowledges it or not, that there is a mandatory set of laws society needs to follow in order to reach the highest levels of productivity and purpose.

In order to understand what that purpose is, we 1st have to take a look at what society is...

CHAPTER TWO

<u>Society Defined</u>

What is a society? At 1st glance, it sounds like a simple question that has been answered a million times before and doesn't need to be defined again. I'm saying it does. Here's why...

Your view on what a society is matters. The view that a society is simply a group of humans coexisting because of their proximity to each other, in my view that would be wrong. It goes deeper than that.

Location is not the basis of society. That view creates too many loopholes and opens humanity up to way too many modes of operating together under one umbrella. To be more specific, I'm saying humanity should be viewed as one, large, global society for all intents and purposes. Why divide it?

All humans live on one planet; therefore, all humans should be operating with the same, general, socially beneficial views of operation. Once society is split apart and broken off into different factions, the universal laws that should govern humanity are thrown out the window and replaced with local and territorial laws. These laws are typically established and enforced for the gain of individual societies and more specifically put, for the gain of *certain individuals* in *certain* societies.

It is a discredit to humanity to view society as anything less than one, global civilization whose goals and intents should result in a concerted effort of human beings living together with the common goal of advancing itself as a whole.

In my view, purpose is the foundation of society. There is a definite hierarchy of life on planet Earth. It is obvious by human's design that we are at the top of the food chain and as being such, we have to operate in a way that is managerially responsible; taking into account the value of all forms of life on Earth, as well as the value of all non-living, natural resources and elements.

That being said, the conversation should organically shift to clearly defining what our role as humans in society should be, operating as a whole unit. That was just a fancy way of describing accountability and that is the topic of the next chapter...

CHAPTER THREE

Accountability Defined

Accountability is all about being submissive and submissive is all about being respectful and being respectful is all about being accountable. See how that circle works?

Accountability is not the cuss-word a lot of members in society would like us to believe. Taken in its' purest definition and form, accountability is an essential element and aspect in all of life.

Look at your home structure. There is a level of accountability that is expected from one family member to the next. When accountability is taken into consideration based on member ranking and position in the family, there is law and order. Chaos reigns supreme when there is a lack of accountability in the home.

Accountability simply acknowledges law, order and respect. It is an excellent governing tool. When accountability is applied to the corporate world, for instance, it means corporations, during their course of doing business, must conduct their operations on a level that is respectful to everyone and everything it is involved in.

That is where the concept of "corporate accountability" stems from. Well, it doesn't stem from corporations in the business sense. The term "corporate" also can mean a group, like a society.

In the business use of corporate accountability, it means there is an established set of laws society has put in place to make sure corporations aren't polluting the water, for instance.

In the societal use of corporate accountability, it means there is an established set of laws society has put in place to make sure individuals aren't acting in a way that is detrimental or impeding to other members of society in their daily routines.

Either way you look at it, accountability is the establishment of order. It can be done through external or internal forces. By external forces, I'm referring to governmental compliance. Like I said, that's when the government steps in and keeps an eye on business activity to make sure they are keeping everything kosher in regards to their effect on government as well as how they present their financial standings.

There is a common thought among business leaders that the act of being accountable is a good thing...so long as each industry is able to establish its' own rules of accountability. Actually, that isn't much different than the way a lot of members in society view accountability.

Societal members seem to all have a sense of "I can do what I like as long as it feels good to me and I'm not directly or intentionally hurting anybody else in a physical or financial way. In society, we tend to want to rely on our own internal accountability controls…but our prison system tends to show proof to the contrary.

Anyways, accountability is an essential and mandatory part of society. In my view, it is the glue that holds society together. So, if I believe it is society's glue and backbone, then I must also believe there is a right or a wrong way to establish it in society, right? If you asked that question you would be exactly right and that leads us into the principles of "Yff's Theory of Mandatory Social Accountability"…

CHAPTER FOUR

<u>The 3 Principles Defined</u>

My Theory is based on principles that are undeniable. In life, there are principles based on facts, some based on personal experience and others based on a combination of the two. The principles I am about to share with you have nothing to do with what I think, feel, know or have experienced: they are based purely on indisputable facts. Here they are:

Principle One: Design in Nature

There is unmistakable design in nature. There is absolutely no way any rationale, sane individual can look at nature and claim it just happened. If you disagree with me, does that mean I am saying you are stupid? No, but I am saying you have to be an irrational, insane individual if you can't see the design in nature.

Design in Nature is the 1st principle because it establishes something very important: a designer. Once again, I am not going to say who the designer is. That is up to each of you to decide for yourself BUT at the same time, your quality of life and the quality of life for humanity as a whole can all be traced to who you and humanity say the designer is.

I've said this before that there are thousands of planets in the universe. There is only 1 that resembles Earth.

There is only 1 planet out of thousands, and some scientists say millions, of planets that has an ozone layer. If there is no ozone layer, there is no life.

There is only 1 planet out of thousands, and some scientists say millions, of planets that has an ozone layer and water. If there is no ozone layer or water, there is no life.

There is only 1 planet out of thousands, and some scientists say millions, of planets that has an ozone layer, water and is the exact distance it needs to be from the sun. If Earth was a little closer to the Sun it would burn up and if it was a little farther away it would freeze.

I could go on into a billion examples of all the "coincidences" that had to be in place for us to live on Earth, but I won't. It should be obvious based on scientific evidence that there is a definite design and uniqueness to planet Earth.

Who designed it? We as humans need to be accountable to whoever the designer is. Why? Because the designer designed it! Humans don't have the capacity to design planets. We did not design the natural laws of gravity or any other natural laws: we have to follow them. We are held in check by the laws that were put in place on Earth, laws that a designer placed here.

We as humans cannot escape nature's laws no matter how hard we try. In fact, our bodies are designed to naturally function on this planet and this planet only! Our design is only suitable for life on Earth in our most natural form.

Could we naturally live on other planets? Potentially, but in order to do so, there has to be a whole lot of environmental changes that must take place 1st. And I'm talking about changing the air somehow, creating natural planetary water sources somehow, creating natural elements in the soil to grow plants somehow…

My point is, why go through all of that when it's obvious that our human design is perfectly and intentionally suited for life on planet Earth? And that leads us to the second principle…

Principle Two: Design in Humans

Humans all have the same basic design. The working aspects of our design are definitely the same; while the external features of our design is where all of the noticeable differences such as skin color, eye color, hair color, height, body types and other individual characteristics can be seen.

In reality, the external human characteristics have very little to do with our common, internal functions. All humans are designed with lungs, eyes, brains, muscle tissue, blood, sexual organs, etc. The design in all humans is to be able to live on planet Earth. It doesn't matter what argument you can come up with, you can not dispute the fact that all humans are made with the same basic chemistry and physical bodies and that that design is only suitable for life on Earth...none of the other thousands or millions of planets we know or don't know about.

This brings me to a quick side point. I was discussing my theory with a guy I know and he is an atheist. He said he does not believe God made everything but he does believe with 100% confidence that somebody did. Where we differed in views was that while I claim God is the designer and that He has a specific plan for humans and Earth, he disagreed.

He wanted to focus on the fact that there are millions of planets out there that we haven't been able to look at closely and that there might be life on one of those or that there might be water and plants on one of those.

I am open to possibilities and I have been known to play poker, shoot dice and buy lotter tickets BUT to me, withholding credit to God as being the designer simply based on the fact that humans may not be as special as the Bible says we are because there MIGHT be, a million light years away, a planet where there MIGHT be water and there MIGHT be some form of life is insane!

Why waste a lifetime focusing on what MIGHT be out there in the universe that humans MIGHT discover 10,000 years from now? Why not focus on what we do know about right here and now: we live on planet Earth and it's designed around us and we are designed around it? Him and I have agreed to disagree. Back to the principle...

It is clear that humans were designed to function only on planet Earth. It is also clear that humans are designed to be the most intelligent and highest life form on Earth. Acknowledging intentional and unique design in both nature and humanity leads us to the 3rd principle...

Principle Three: Responsibility

Acknowledging there is a designer of both nature and humanity, it becomes clear that humans need to act responsibly. That is where our societies can't seem to agree on and where I say our place of agreement should be in unison and obvious by nature.

There is a designer. Whenever somebody designs something, they know what's best for it. You design something intentionally. With a purpose. All design has a purpose. Where there is no design there is chaos and chaos has no purpose. There is definite purpose in the design in nature and humanity, the problem is getting everybody in society to agree on what that purpose is. It's not like we humans haven't tried.

There are societies set up that claim to be free and democratic. In these societies, the laws of the land change every time the wind blows. When one political party is in office the laws are one way and when the other political party is in office the laws go a different way.

It's a never-ending cycle of greed and stupidity. One party blames the other party for the wrongs in society and they begin to position themselves to control national policy; while the other party is focused on making moves to keep it and its' policies the law of the land.

Then there are societies run by a monarchy. The King or Queen says what the law is and there is nobody who can test it. The King of Queen owns all of the riches of the government and nobody can test it.

In both forms of society, the goal is control. The ultimate goal is to gain legal control over society so that it 1) is determined by the ruling party and 2) allows the ruling party to maintain control and 3) be to the financial benefit of the ruling party.

You see, when society is broken down and fragmented out, each society can determine its' own laws. These laws are designed to benefit only a few. The governing view of members in a society are based on greed, control and pride.

Society has taken it upon itself to determine what the laws of operation should be with no regard to the designer. The responsibility of lawmakers in society should be in alignment with the laws and designs of nature and humanity. When humanity is seen as one, big, global entity, that law will be established for the benefit of one, big, global entity. It's when societies create their own physical boundaries that chaos erupts.

Responsibility. The creation must be responsible to the creator. The creator has the design. The creator has the vision. The creator has the purpose. The creator can see the big picture. The creator operates on a higher intelligence level than the creation.

We as humans need to act in a way that is responsible. When we act in ways that our irresponsible it shows. We don't function as one, big, global entity. We all need to be on the same page and that takes us to the summarization of "Yff's Theory of Mandatory Social Accountability"...

"Yff's Theory of Mandatory Social Accountability" states that:

1. There is only one society and it is called civilization.

2. All members of the global society called civilization are created equal in design and capacity.

3. All members of civilization have the same design source.

4. In order to achieve civilization's maximum, socially beneficial objectives and purposes, it must, as one body, act in a responsible manner and hold itself accountable to the laws and designs in both nature and humanity as laid out by the designer.

5. Adherence to the designer's laws in every aspect of life is mandatory and each member must be held accountable to it without exception or prejudice.

SUMMARY

For myself, I had to learn how to be accountable to a Higher Power. It was obvious that I, as a human, did not design myself, humanity or planet Earth. Acknowledging that was my first step in developing my theory that got me on a better track in life.

Even though my theory is not based on my own thoughts or experiences, I was able to use the principles in it to establish a way of life that made me a more productive member in this global society called civilization; while allowing me to find my individual purpose in life.

For myself, I have applied this Theory to the Bible and the belief that God is the designer of everything seen and unseen. That being established, it became mandatory that I followed His rules. Following His rules has led me to be able to respectfully appreciate everyone else's choices for their own rules of conduct in life without hindering my choice.

I encourage you to find a way of life that allows you to apply this Theory as well.

Private Matter Bonus Essays

TOILET PAPER & TELEPHONES

What do you think when you read the title of this essay? At 1st glance you may think it's about talkin' shit, maybe. I mean, you got toilet paper for after you, you know what...and then you have a telephone to talk...

If you thought I would just be talkin' shit, you are wrong. I am thankful for toilet paper and telephones. That got me to thinking: all of the materials to make toilet paper and telephones was here on Earth way before they were produced. Sound boring? Take another look…

We all know there is a lot of design, law and order in nature. Somebody did a whole lot of planning in making this planet and this universe. We all know humans did not make this planet, so that means there is a 100% probability that someone out there is operating on a thought level way above our pay grade.

Toilet paper is made from paper and paper is made from trees and trees need water, dirt and sunlight to grow. If you take away any one of these elements, there is no toilet paper. Whoever designed this planet did some good-ass planning: the designer knew we humans would eventually want to wipe our asses with something softer than maple leaves or whatever they used before Charmin came around.

That's planning; especially considering how some scientist like to say the Earth was made billions of years ago. That means all the ingredients for toilet paper were put on Earth billions of years ago to be available for us to use in our lifetime.

The same can be said for the materials to make telephones, cars, bombs, windows, computers, dog food, baseball bats, pretty much everything and anything on this planet had all the materials to produce it on the Earth millions of years before any of those things were thought of. Do you now see where I'm going with this?

I believe God is the designer of the universe. With that belief, I am publicly saying He is an awesome planner and designer. He made sure everything humans would need was on this planet thousands, or millions of years ago when He made it.

Once I came to that realization, I began to trust and follow every, single plan He had and has for my life. There is no way I can make a plan today that would be fulfilled thousands of years from now. I don't have that ability. No human does.

I think it's time for us humans to humble ourselves and admit 1) there is a higher, more intelligent life form out there and 2) that life form needs to start getting the respect and honor He deserves.

I'm sticking with that life form being God. So, as a mere mortal, I had to stop stealing from Him. I had to stop robbing Him of the respect and honor that is owed to a being who operates on the level God does.

For me, that started with thanking Him for toilet

paper and telephones.

FATHER TIME

Contrary to popular opinion, when God asked the question, "Would a mere mortal, a man, rob God?" I think it had less to do with money and more to do with time. Pastors love to quote this verse in attempts to make the congregation feel guilt. It's as though the pastor is like, "Hey! You better pay attention and stop stealing from God! God doesn't like it when you don't tithe, in fact, He makes it clear you are supposed to give the full amount of your tithe! So, stop stealing from God and dig as deep as your ass can in them pockets and put it in the plate! Thief!"

That passage about stealing from God comes from Malachi 3. God does say we are robbing Him when we don't bring our tithe BUT if you look at Malachi 1, you find the real reason behind tithing that interests Him...

In Malachi 1 God says, "A son honors his father, and a slave honors his master. If I am a father, where is the honor due me? If I am a master, where is the respect due me?"

In my view, when God says, "...where is the honor and respect due me?" He is considering THAT robbery. NOT giving God the honor and respect that you owe Him is stealing from Him. When you don't tithe, you aren't respecting or honoring His laws and when you don't respect someone's laws that means you don't respect them. And when you don't respect them, you are basically stealing from them. You are not giving them what you owe them.

Money is simply a tool to measure time. You work or invest your time and experiences that you've gathered over your life, and you receive money in return. Money is only a physical rendering of time. Money takes time from being something you can't see, to something you can physically see and measure.

When you give money in the collection plate, you are giving time. If you have a lot of money, that means a lot of people have invested their time and purchased something from you with money. In essence, you are now responsible for their time. You are a time-manager. What are you going to do with all the time you have?

Are you going to take all of their time and buy yourself a new yacht each year? Are you going to use their time to buy drugs and get drunk? Are you going to use that time to make sure you and your family alone are taken care of?

We are managers of this Earth. When we give tithe, in my view, it is symbolically acknowledging God's system of management He trusted us with and that is giving God the honor and respect He is due.

So, are we supposed to bring money to the church? Yes. But it's the symbolism behind the money...not the currency value of it.

I think it's time pastors started learning about the principles behind the actions necessary to represent the kingdom of Heaven...and that's my view.

Finding Success the Natural Way

I love to watch documentaries about animals; especially the ones about lions and tigers. For some reason I especially love to watch the life and death aspect of their lives. When I see a group of female lions getting their asses beat, I get excited. I usually get excited for one of two reasons. The first reason is because in my YouTube video search box I typed in, "male lion attacking hyenas" and I already know what's basically going to happen and the second reason is because I have probably already watched the video a hundred times already and I already know *exactly* what's going to happen.

What's going to happen is one male lion, who is twice as big as the lionesses, is going to hear the growls and cries of pain from his lionesses and he is going to storm on the scene like a runaway freight train! He's going to grab a hyena and go straight for the jugular! Whatever hyena he attacks will be breathing its' last breathes and I love it!

I had to finally ask myself why do I like to watch lions and tigers kill or be killed so much? I believe I have my found my answer, as well as a fairly reasonable explanation for my repetitive video-watching behavior, and it's simple.

SUCCESS. That's all it is. As a human, I want to be successful. I want to be able to do exactly what the fuck I was designed to do. I want to be able to live on this planet in a way that is stress free. I want to wake up every, single, mutha fuckin' day and be excited to be alive! I want success! What does that have to do with lions and tigers? Everything.

You see, when I watch documentaries and videos about lions and tigers, I am watching them do exactly what it is they were designed to do. They are called carnivores because they eat meat. How do they eat meat? Their eyes are positioned on their heads in such a way that they can lay low in the grass and still see the prey they are stalking. They have big ass paws with big ass claws that they will use when they jump on their prey. Once the prey is secured in place by the claws digging into its' torso, the big cat sinks its' 3-inch, sharp-as-knives, canine teeth into whatever body part is the closest. Once the prey animal has begun to panic and slow down, the lion or tiger finds its way to the victim's throat and bites down on it, suffocating the animal to death. At this point, the attack animal's victim doesn't have a prayer. It will begin to be eaten whether it's fully dead or still alive and I love that shit!

It's a typical success scene in nature and it's what we love to see and it's what we all want to experience. Lions and tigers are predators and are built to hunt and kill and when they are doing that, they are doing what they were designed to do and there is something beautiful to see both humans and nature doing what they were designed to do. There is a sort of beauty and awe in it. I'm sure the prey animals don't think so, but even them, they are doing what they were designed to do and there is a natural beauty in that as well. You can't have carnivores without plant-eating herbivores. And if you didn't have carnivores, the herbivores numbers would swell and then they would all die because since they all eat the same grass which has a limited supply, there won't be enough to feed all of them.

Even though I like to watch the big cats, it's to the point where some of the videos get me so emotional and mad that I can't watch them and that's not a good thing. It drives me absolutely crazy because I know the wildlife photographers and safari guides are supposed to get as close to the action as possible to 1) make as much money from safari tours as they can and 2) provide us with endless hours of real life animal action but still...I literally hate it and cannot watch a video where a lion is getting ready to do what it does and the safari guide has its big, bright ass light shining right on the lion, giving its position away or is driving damn near right alongside the lion just so the paying tourists can feel like they have gotten their money's worth.

I'm like, "Get the fuck out of their way!" "Stop being so close to them! Give them some space and let them breathe!" "How is he supposed to make a kill when there's 20 fucking safari trucks circling the action?!?" I literally turn the tv off and start doing pushups to take some stress off. I even have to make sure I don't talk to anybody or send an email off until I've had time to decompress properly or I might say or email off the wrong shit.

It's as though it's naturally in me to despise it when anything or anyone isn't able to freely do what it is in life. This drive for success in humans can take on some crazy forms. This drive for success is what makes us commit suicide when we don't feel successful. This drive for success makes us rob and steal from other people just so we can get what we want and feel successful. This drive makes us kill each other out of greed. This drive makes us want to do whatever it takes to get money because we feel like having money means success; and at the worst-case scenario, if we are not driven by money, we know we have to have at least a base amount to be able to survive from day to day.

I know this young buck who wants to flip houses. When I asked him why he said, "That's where the money is." And this is the part where I tie God and the Bible into this Private Matter.

If you acknowledge the facts that there is definitely natural design in life and nature and that somebody designed it, the odds of you finding success in the way it was tailor-made for you personally increases dramatically.

I believe God created everything we see and don't see. Knowing this, if He is the designer, I need to contact Him and see what His plans are for my life. The Bible is a history/law book that teaches us who God is, how we can be in contact with Him and provides plenty of examples of real-life people who were able to find their individual access by tapping into God.

I found it and I love sharing with people how it works as I go through the process. I know there aren't many examples in the upper levels of society where we see people giving God glory for their personal or financial success, but don't let that stop you. If you aren't seeing examples of humans doing what they were designed by God to do, face your life-camera to a different direction and look at nature.

In nature you will find a gazillion examples of success the way God designed it. You will see birds flying and it will give you an inner peace. It will give you a peace because even though watching a bird fly is a simple thing. Maybe you will start to see the beauty in it. Watch a spider catch something in its web. Spiders have webs that, if they were in the human world, would be 50 times more powerful than any human-made material. Spiders naturally design different types of webs and they come with different types of venom.

Animals have God-designed weapons and skills. Each set of weapons and/or skills is designed to help each type of animal find success. After reading this Private Matter topic, I really hope you take the time to watch an animal documentary, I personally and highly recommend Big Cat videos, and look at how they are simply doing what they were designed to do.

Watching these videos might inspire you. If you're not a big animal-documentary-watcher, just watch your dog doing what it naturally likes to do and see how happy it is doing shit like licking its ass and balls or excitedly chasing its tail for 30 minutes. Watch how a baby naturally get excited just seeing you smile at it. Watch how a cat loves to irritate you by rubbing itself against your face while you sleep...knowing you are allergic to its ass. I'm a dog person but I have to admit cats are super smart...and sneaky.

It might help you properly channel that inner-drive you have for success. It might help you want to see what God, the greatest designer ever, has designed and planned for your life. Finding your personalized plan based on your design and skill will naturally lower your stress level.

You won't know until you take a look at your life from a God-design viewpoint. Your view matters, finding your God-designed purpose in life matters and you matter.

Personal Development Notes

Personal Development Notes

45

Personal Development Notes

Personal Development Notes

47

Personal Development Notes

Personal Development Notes